D.I.Y. MAKE IT HAPPEN

DOG-WALKING BUSINESS

VIRGINIA LOH-HAGAN

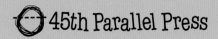

45th Parallel Press

Published in the United States of America by Cherry Lake Publishing
Ann Arbor, Michigan
www.cherrylakepublishing.com

Reading Adviser: Marla Conn, ReadAbility, Inc.
Book Designer: Felicia Macheske

45th Parallel Press is an imprint of Cherry Lake Publishing.

Library of Congress Cataloging-in-Publication Data

Names: Loh-Hagan, Virginia, author.
Title: Dog-walking business / by Virginia Loh-Hagan.
Description: Ann Arbor : Cherry Lake Publishing, [2016] | Series: D.I.Y. Make
 it happen | Includes bibliographical references and index.
Identifiers: LCCN 2015026843| ISBN 9781634704977 (hardcover) | ISBN
 9781634706179 (pbk.) | ISBN 9781634705578 (pdf) | ISBN 9781634706773
 (ebook)
Subjects: LCSH: Dog walking—Juvenile literature. | Dogs—Services
 for—Juvenile literature. | Home-based businesses—Juvenile literature.
Classification: LCC SF427.46 .L64 2016 | DDC 636.7/083--dc23
LC record available at http://lccn.loc.gov/2015026843

Cherry Lake Publishing would like to acknowledge the work of The Partnership for 21st Century Skills.
Please visit *www.p21.org* for more information.

Printed in the United States of America
Corporate Graphics Inc.

ABOUT THE AUTHOR

Dr. Virginia Loh-Hagan is an author, university professor, former classroom teacher, and curriculum designer. She lives in San Diego with her very tall husband and very naughty dogs. Every morning, her husband walks their dogs around the park. People feed them treats. Everyone knows the dogs. To learn more about her, visit www.virginialoh.com.

TABLE OF CONTENTS

CHAPTER ONE

WHAT DOES IT MEAN TO START A DOG-WALKING BUSINESS?

Do you love dogs? Do you love being outside? Then, starting a dog-walking business is the right project for you!

Dogs need to be walked every day. They need exercise. They need to go to the bathroom. But dog owners work. They go on trips. They're busy. They need help. So they hire dog walkers. Dog walkers take care of dogs. They walk the dogs. They let the dogs out.

Dog walkers work every day. They're most busy during the workweek. But they also work weekends. They work holidays. They work in any kind of weather.

Talk to other dog walkers.
Get tips from them.

KNOW THE LINGO

Alpha: a dog that is dominant or in charge

Bait: food or toy used to get a dog's attention

Choke: a collar with a straight piece of material joined by looping it through one or two rings on each end

Crate: a container to transport dogs

Croup: the area from the back of the dog's hip to the root of the tail

Cue: request for your dog to do something

Gait: how a dog moves

Master the walk: the dog walks next to you or behind you, and is not pulling ahead

Pack leader: alpha dog

Roadwork: exercising a dog by walking, jogging, or biking

Shift dogs: dogs that you walk a few times a week because of clients' work schedules

Socializing: helping dogs get along with people and other dogs

Temperament: a dog's personality

Withers: highest point between the dog's shoulders

A dog-walking **business** means you make money. People buy and sell **services**. A service is something you do for someone. Dog walkers provide a service. They walk dogs for **clients**. Clients pay them. Clients are dog owners. Clients trust dog walkers. They let them in their homes. They let them walk their dogs.

Dog walkers charge $10 to $20 an hour per dog. They usually walk three to five dogs at a time. This means they make a good hourly rate.

A dog-walking business is a good idea. You'll make money. You'll get exercise. You'll get fresh air. You get to hang out with dogs! Start a dog-walking business whenever you want. Dog walkers are needed all the time!

Start with one dog. Then see how you handle multiple dogs.

CHAPTER TWO

WHAT DO YOU NEED TO START A DOG-WALKING BUSINESS?

Think about how you want to be known.

➡ **Come up with several names for your business.**

➡ **Think of fun names.**

➡ **Relate the names to dogs.**

➡ **Choose the best name.**

➡ **Design a logo. A logo is a picture. It matches your name. It lets people know what you do. Ask an artistic friend for help.**

Clients need to be able to contact you.

➡ **Give clients you know your phone number.**

➡ **Create an e-mail account. This e-mail should be for business only.**

➡ **Create a Web site.**

➡ **Create business cards. These cards have your contact information.**

Put your business name and logo on everything.

You'll need several things.

➡ Get poop bags.

➡ Get a **portable** water bowl. That's a bowl that folds up.

➡ Get a water bottle. Some places don't have water.

➡ Get extra leashes. Get extra collars. Dogs will have their own. But you should be prepared.

➡ Get a **muzzle**. This goes over a dog's mouth. Some dogs may not be nice.

➡ Get towels. Dogs may get dirty. You'll want to clean them.

➡ Get good walking shoes. You'll be walking a lot.

➡ Get a dog **first-aid** kit. Dogs may get cuts.

➡ Get dog treats. You'll want to reward dogs.

➡ Get a backpack. Your hands will hold leashes. Carry things on your back.

You can use plastic grocery bags as poop bags.

You need to love dogs. You need to know about dogs.

➡ Learn about different dog **breeds**. Breeds are dog types.

➡ Learn about dog behavior.

➡ Learn about dog body language.

➡ Learn how to handle dogs.

➡ Learn basic dog-training skills.

➡ Learn how to handle dog **emergencies**. An emergency is when something dangerous happens. An example is choking.

➡ Learn where you can walk dogs.

There are different ways you can learn about dogs.

➡ **Read books.**

➡ **Read Internet articles.**

➡ **Watch videos.**

➡ **Help at a dog shelter. Some dogs don't have homes. A shelter takes care of these dogs.**

➡ **Take dog-training classes.**

Take a pet first-aid class.

TRY THIS!

A dog walker walks dogs outside. Sometimes, the weather is bad. It rains. It snows. But dogs still need exercise. So, dog walkers need to get creative. Create an obstacle course for your dog. Obstacles are objects. An obstacle course is like a fun race. Your dog goes from one point to another. The dog has to get over the obstacles.

You'll need: treats, obstacles.

Steps

1 Ask dog owners if it's okay to exercise their dog inside.

2 Pick a room of the house.

3 Move objects around. Place them so the dog can move through the objects.

4 Hide treats in different places.

5 Give the dog a treat.

6 Lead the dog to the first obstacle. Let the dog find the rest of the treats.

7 Watch the dog. Make sure nothing gets damaged.

8 Clean up. Make sure the room looks like it did before the obstacle course.

Ask family to help you take care of business matters.

Starting a business is more than walking dogs. You'll need to take care of paperwork.

➡ **Learn about accounting. Keep track of your money. You spend money. You make money. Businesses make a profit. The money you earned pays for expenses. Profit is the money that's left over.**

➡ **Learn about marketing. Let people know about you. This is how you'll get clients.**

➡ **Check with your city. You might need a business permit. A permit allows you to do something.**

➡ **Check about insurance. This is protection. Accidents happen.**

➡ **Check about taxes. A tax is money paid to the government.**

CHAPTER THREE

HOW DO YOU SET UP A DOG-WALKING BUSINESS?

You want to walk dogs every day. You want to walk several groups of dogs. Each group should have two to three dogs. You need clients. You need to market your business.

➡ Create posters. Put them in pet shops. Put them in pet hospitals. Put them at dog parks.

➡ Talk to a vet. A vet is an animal doctor. Vets will tell clients about you.

➡ List your business on dog and pet Web sites.

➡ Make friends with other dog walkers. They may need you to fill in for them. They may have too many clients. They may want to go on vacation.

JESSICA DOLCE

Jessica Dolce is a professional dog walker. She lives in Maine. She lives with two dogs, three cats, and her husband. She's walked dogs for more than 10 years. She walks up to 50 dogs a week. She came up with DINOS. It stands for Dogs in Need of Space. Not all dogs like other dogs or people. She advises asking permission before going up to a dog. She said, "It's nothing personal. It's just about space!" Dolce also advises dog walkers to be responsible. She said, "You better be trustworthy. Really trustworthy. Never take it for granted how much your clients trust you to always be doing the right thing in their homes and with their pets. Most of your clients will really appreciate you and value your role in their lives. Don't blow it. … It's a really cool thing to be a dog's favorite person (aside from their owners, of course)."

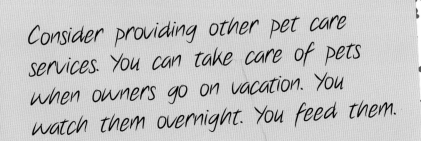

Consider providing other pet care services. You can take care of pets when owners go on vacation. You watch them overnight. You feed them.

Develop a plan to keep track of your clients. Remember, your clients are dog owners. Your clients are also dogs. Learn all you can about the owners and the dogs.

➡ **Note their names.**

➡ **Note where they live. Note where they usually walk.**

➡ **Note their phone numbers. Get a phone number for the vet.**

➡ **Note their rules. Some owners have special ways of doing things. Ask about treats.**

➡ **Note the dog's habits.**

➡ **Note the dog's interests.**

➡ **Note the dog's allergies. These are things that bother them. An example is grass.**

➡ **Note the dog's health. Make sure dogs have had their shots. Make sure dogs don't have fleas.**

➡ **Make a ring of cards. Each card has client information. Take this with you.**

Make sure dogs are healthy. You don't want them getting other dogs sick.

Develop a plan for getting paid.

➡ **Decide your** fees**. A fee is how much you'll charge. Most dog walkers charge per hour. Some charge extra. They charge per dog.**

➡ **Decide what happens if clients cancel. Things come up. Ask clients to give you a day's notice. Otherwise, you'll charge them.**

➡ **Create** contracts**. A contract is an agreement. It says clients will pay you. And you will walk their dogs.**

➡ **Decide how you'll collect money. Some dog walkers collect money each week. Some collect after each job.**

➡ **Give clients an** invoice**. It's a note. It lets clients know how much money they owe.**

Develop a scheduling plan.

➡ **Get a calendar.**

➡ **Plan your jobs.**

➡ **Be on time. Clients are counting on you. Dogs need to go to the bathroom.**

Walk dogs in your neighborhood.

Learn how to walk more than one dog at a time. Only walk dogs you can control. Practice dog walking.

➡ **Prepare your leashes. Put your wrist through all leash loops. Grab the leashes about a foot down from your hand. Dogs pull. This helps you keep control.**

➡ **Keep moving. Keep your pace. Dogs get distracted. Ignore things that pull dogs away.**

➡ **Watch all dogs.**

➡ **Don't pull. The more you pull them, they'll pull you. Relax. Try to keep the leashes loose.**

➡ **Walk a dog by itself. Then, add dogs to the pack. A pack is a group of dogs.**

Try to use a harness. It's easier than a collar.

CHAPTER FOUR

HOW DO YOU RUN A DOG-WALKING BUSINESS?

You've got a business. You've got dogs. You're ready to get going!

There are things you need to do before walking the dog.

➡ **Visit the dog with the owner. Do this before you walk the dog on your own. Get to know the dog. Play with the dog. Go over details with the owner. Get your clients to trust you.**

➡ **Make sure you know everything about the dog.**

➡ **Set up dog-walking times.**

➡ **Discuss how you're getting the dogs. Some clients give dog walkers house keys. Some clients leave extra keys in a special place. Some clients leave the house unlocked.**

Write all the details down in your contract.

QUICK TIPS

- These are the most basic dog commands: sit, lie down, stay, come, leave it, drop it, wait, heel, and focus.

- Don't accept treats from strangers. People have given poisoned treats to dogs. Some dogs have allergies.

- Some dog walkers provide dog-running services. Dog runners run with dogs for 1 to 10 miles (1.6 to 16 kilometers). They don't run with more than two dogs at a time.

- Get off your phone. Don't talk and walk. Be with the dogs.

- Keep dogs on leashes. Letting dogs run off-leash is risky.

- You spend time not walking. You go to the house. You go from place to place. You don't get paid for this time. So focus on a small part of town.

- Don't be afraid of poop. You will get poop on you. Wipe it off with grass.

There are things you need to do when you go dog walking.

- ➡ Be on time. Remember, clients are counting on you. The dog needs you.

- ➡ Let yourself in the house. (Keep your clients' keys in a safe place.)

- ➡ Greet the dog. Let it smell you. Let it lick you. Pet the dog.

- ➡ Make sure you have your backpack.

- ➡ Prepare the dog. Put on its leash.

- ➡ Walk the dog.

- ➡ Let it use the bathroom. Pick up its poop. Use the bag. Scoop it up. Throw the bag away.

- ➡ Clean the dog. Dogs may roll in stuff. Dogs may step in stuff.

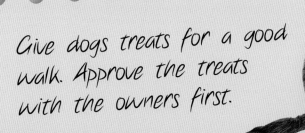

Give dogs treats for a good walk. Approve the treats with the owners first.

There may be times when you can't walk the dog. You may get sick. You may go on vacation.

➡ **Tell your clients. Let them know a week ahead of time.**

➡ **Ask another dog walker to fill in.**

➡ **Train another person to help you.**

Ask clients to recommend your business. They tell other people. They promote you.

There are things you need to do after dog walking.

➡ **Collect your money.**

➡ **Give clients a report. Let them know about their dogs.**

➡ **Ask clients for good comments.**

➡ **Ask clients what you can improve.**

➡ **Thank clients.**

Starting a dog-walking business is a lot of work. But it's also a lot of fun. You get to play with dogs. You get to make some money. You get to help your community.

WOOF
WOOF

D.I.Y. EXAMPLE!

STEPS	EXAMPLES
Name	Furry Feet Services
Services	• Walk one or two dogs at a time • Vacation pet sitting: three daily visits including a walk • Clean dog feet after every walk • Free dog treats
Marketing plan	Signs at the local library
Fees	• $12 for 30 minutes • $40 for vacation pet sitting • One free dog walk for every 15 walks • One free dog walk for every new client

STEPS	EXAMPLES
Pack backpack	◆ Poop bags or plastic grocery bags
	◆ Portable water bowl
	◆ Water bottle
	◆ Different sizes of leashes
	◆ Collar
	◆ Harness
	◆ Muzzle
	◆ Towels
	◆ Baby wipes
	◆ Dog treats
	◆ First-aid kit: bandages, tape, healing cream
Where	◆ Neighborhood
	◆ City park

GLOSSARY

accounting (uh-KOUNT-ing) keeping track of money

allergies (AL-ur-jeez) things that cause a reaction in people and animals

breeds (BREEDZ) dog types

business (BIZ-nis) an organization that provides a service and makes money

clients (KLYE-uhnts) people who hire a dog walker; dog owners

contracts (KAHN-trakts) agreements

emergencies (ih-MUR-juhn-seez) things that are dangerous, like choking or fire

fees (FEEZ) costs

first aid (FURST AYD) help given to people or dogs who hurt themselves before medical help can be provided

insurance (in-SHOOR-uhns) protection in case something bad happens

invoice (IN-vois) a note that states how much money a client owes

logo (LOH-goh) a picture that represents a business

marketing (MAHR-kit-ing) promoting a business

muzzle (MUHZ-uhl) a cover that goes over a dog's mouth

pack (PAK) a group of dogs

permit (PUR-mit) a document that gives you permission to do something

portable (POR-tuh-buhl) something that can be easily moved

profit (PRAH-fit) the money you earned that's left over after paying for all your expenses

services (SUR-vis-iz) things that are provided to someone else

shelter (SHEL-tur) a place that takes care of dogs without homes

taxes (TAKS-ez) fees paid to the government

vet (VET) animal doctor, short for veterinarian

INDEX

LEARN MORE

BOOKS

Baines, Becky with Gary Weitzman. *Everything Dogs: All the Canine Facts, Photos, and Fun that You Can Get Your Paws On!* Washington, DC: National Geographic Society, 2012.

Royston, Angela. *Diary of a Dog Walker*. Chicago: Heinemann, 2013

WEB SITES

eHow—"How to Start a Dog Walking Business for Kids": www.ehow.com/how_6312374_start-dog-walking-business-kids.html

Kids in Biz—"Dog Walking Service": http://kids-in-biz.com/kib/30/dog-walking-service/

National Association of Professional Pet Sitters: www.petsitters.org